ONLY FEED ME LIFE

by
Jerome Braggs

and illustrated by
Val Ashford

Only Feed Me Life

Copyright © 2024 Jerome Braggs

All rights reserved.

ISBN: 979-8-218-36532-5

"The poet, when effective, is not merely a writer of words, but a cultural worker — a healer who uses the alchemy of language to mend the broken and bind the wounds of our collective spirit."

-Bobby LeFebre

for all those who loved me —
whether in my family, in my friendships, in my relationships, in my work, in the hospital, or in the dialysis clinic, please know: you helped remind me that this life of mine is a poem worth writing.
thank you

Chapters

ONLY FEED ME LIFE

life lessons.

today, while sitting down to decide the title of this book

i found a title i loved

one that breathed itself into my lungs
when i spoke it

one that illuminated the
irises of my eyes when i heard it's
name riding the currents of the air

one that lifted my back straight
and relaxed my shoulders
slowed my breathing
and settled in to the muscles of my body
in a way that let me know
that the sound of it

feels like home

but
then

i got to thinking about
what you would think about it

how would it settle in your body
to hear

how would your lungs expand
as you breathed it in
would your heart know that it was home, too

funny, how often i determine what gets to feed me
by seeing if it would also feed you

it seems, sometimes, i can't let myself eat my own joy

i can't just sit inside the circumference of what breaths
life into my own lungs

without first, making sure you are breathing, too

that you, too, would eat my joy
that you, too, would find it delicious

it's in this small way i think i have starved myself
of my own happiness

kept myself from eating the joy that was meant to be served
only on my plate

instead, i take it off, and try and mold it so that it fits prettily
on yours

you must be able to eat it, too
or else i mustn't

this is illness, i think

to not feel like i can be happy

all alone

to feel my happiness must come after someone else's

but i am worthy of a happiness that doesn't require approval,
or company

to feel good about something
first

alone
by myself

i know this as truth
though i don't always act
like i do

i deserve to choose
the title of this book
because it feels like home to me

even if no one else wants to live there

i had no model for the kind of life i yearned

black.
gay.
man.
hiv+.

there was no one in my direct line of sight that
illuminated the possibility
of the sheer joy
and rest

and aliveness
i wanted

i built this life
in the mud of hope

and blindness,
and rage for having to ride the
back of an irrational faith
that what i am

deserved/belonged
to whatever it felt

possible, calling, delicious

the fact i received
this kind of life
is more than a celebration

it is a creation

i weaved this out of thin air

and stardust, and tears
and examples unseen

let the world tell it
i was not supposed to have

but i have

that is its own kind of magic

having when you ain't supposed to have

i am my own kind of magician

creating what wasn't there with flair
and slights of hand

but i have not come to entertain you
i come to be entertained

clap your hands
dance around me

bow, if you must

for you are witnessing a miracle
in my existence

black
gay
man
hiv+

and alive

happy
rested

not dying, but living

well, better

i ain't supposed to have.
but i have.

i ain't supposed to live,
but i live

juicily

can't you see how beautiful that is?

are you not amused?

failure

it will come

it must

it has been assigned
to break you

drain the planets out of
your eyes

bleed the milky ways
out of your veins

mead and crush
the mountains on which you've

stood for so long

because how else will you get
the transfusion of stars

you so desperately need

to become more of
the light

you must become more

of the light

you must

eventually

hopefully

you get to a point where
you are tired of rejecting yourself

tired of having parts
that aren't ever fed your
own love

tired of feeling like
pieces of you
don't belong,
can't be loved,

aren't safe in this
wide open
world

eventually,
hopefully

you stop waging war
and make peace

with you

and then,
only then

you find out

how fucking beautiful you are,
always been

and how worthy of living
in the light

those pieces + parts are,
have always been

and then,
only then

life becomes delicious

the taste of it
becomes something
peaceful
happy
loving

because it starts bending over
backwards
and sideways
and under

to prove this has always been true

of you
for you

you discover you have
always belonged

because you are loved

lovable
love

i am here to be

happy + loved

an ancient truth
i am starting

to remember

i can remember hearing that

i couldn't get into heaven if i stayed gay

some man in a pulpit who barely knew my name
proclaiming that my love of men would deny me
my right to be loved eternally

and isn't that what we all want?

to be loved…
eternally

but i'm not sure if it's heaven if
everyone i've ever loved isn't there

and i'm not sure if it's hell
if everyone i've loved is there

even if they're in pain
we are there together, sharing the pain

and i'm not sure that's not love
(sharing the pain of those you love)

and i'm not sure that's not heaven
(being surrounded by those you love)

sharing everything with them

even your eternal presence
in the most difficult of times

i've been broken 1000 times

and each time i
built an altar
on the edges of my brokenness

lamenting what was lost

left
denied

today
i am still breaking

but my altar sits
at a different place

on the edge of what
has been broken open

and i celebrate what
has come, birthed,

brought the light

what has been broken
is never as important

as what it has broken
open

for me

sometimes, i wonder what the moon sees

when she sees me

standing there at night

in her light

hoping
for better days

all while she's up there
glowing in all her glory

offering me a damn good night

right in the moment

while i'm too busy wanting
to be somewhere, something else

and ain't noticed a bit

my, my how many gifts go

unnoticed

by impatient men

waiting on more
shiny things to arrive

i am love and light

i am also

you got me
all the way
fucked up.

crisis?

naw i ain't scared of him
we's long time friends

whenever he comes a knockin
i opens the door
says, '*come on in baby
have some tea
you tired?*

*i know you's come a long way
to sit and visit a spell.
you ailing?*

*just lay your head down here
and tell me bout
all the places you been
all the things you seen
all them things you think is real.*'

then i just rocks him
til he falls asleep
and let's me weave a
metamorphosis into him

a newness, a sweetness

on his skin

so he can be real pretty
when he wakes up

but then i wakes up
instead

and realize how silly i been
dreaming i was talking to
crisis

cause when he comes over

he does the talking
and the weaving

and i does the sleeping

and the waking up pretty

i have bills to pay

a lawn to tend to
investments to manage
spreadsheets to create
a body to cherish
relationships to mend

though i am made of heaven
i still have earthly duties

damnit

belovéd

you feel heavy
because you are filled
with secrets

spill them out

let them fall sloppily
into the day

open your mouth
and stain the silence
with your truth

the light was always
supposed to be
home

light was always
how you were

supposed to travel

you were never built
for the heavy
of secrets

i have learned that

focusing on what will make you
lots of money

but not also focusing on

what will bring you
lots of joy

is its own kind of hell

i have spent too much

way too much
time

saving the world

and not enough
not nearly enough
time

saving myself

i traveled many years
unaware

that what the world
was eating from the palms
of my hands

was supposed to
be mine to eat

so many years the world
left from me
well fed

while i left from me
starving

and so confused at why

no more

nevermore

and i do not need
a raven to cry it out
for me

my soul is loud enough

me, to my guides:

what the fuck is going on here?!

them, to me:
if you knew you were loved,
would you keep asking that same question?

me:
apparently not

guides:
then you know what's going on here,

and you know what you must do

i love who i become when

i let go

of things
that are too heavy for me

stress
pushing
forcing
struggling

other people's opinions of me

trying to control what was
never mine to control

there is a lightness
in my body

a peace
in my mind

a freedom in my energy

i feel more at home in
myself

we are never publicly taught

the truth of things
like this

that letting go is medicine
and holding tight is illness

and we are not meant to carry such heavy things

and not meant to travel this life
any other way but light

i love how good i feel when
i let go

i do not want to let go
of the memory of this

but even that, i guess
i must

because i definitely do
at times

sometimes i can forget

that life has
a plan for
my life

a plan for
my highest good

a plan for my
deep joy

a plan for my
greatest wellness

sometimes i can forget
that life actually
loves

me

and that i don't
have to try so

damn hard

to make it

do so

dear black parents...

every time
you tell your
black child

to put their
hands
at 10 and 2

keep their voice low

not cause any waves

you teach them to let their
inner authority die

so that the outer ones can live
instead

which seems like
a great idea

until the day comes

when you realize they
have been waiting their

whole life

for someone else
to tell them

it's safe to be alive

and to drive with abandon
towards the place that holds

their dream

i will not (cannot yet) speak from certainty

that life only gets better
with trusting ourselves

but i can speak from the
marrow in my bones that

life gets worse,
without it.

what does being loved feel like?

he asked me

i don't know
i say

maybe you should ask the desert
what it feels after
a long torrential rain

or the old dog what it feels
when its adopted after years of
sleeping on the cold, stone floor
of the pound

maybe
i say

it feels like knowing
i finally belong
here

in this moment

with everything there is
in me

with everything there isn't
in me

i think that's it
i say

being loved feels like knowing
i belong to everything this moment
has to offer

and letting it hold me

wrap me and show me

that i'm not wrong
for wanting to surrender to it

what is surrender?

surrender is an act of self-care

it says:
even if this doesn't change,
i deserve peace

surrender is an act of worthiness

it says:
i deserve to not have to figure this out on my own,
so i won't

surrender is an act of romance

it says:
make love to me as i let go

surrender is an act of welcome

it says:
please tell me what you need from me
so that you feel safe enough here to
give me the gift
you have for me
hidden within you

surrender is an act of gratitude

it says:
yes, and *thank you......*
even if i can't see why right now

surrender is an act of manifestation

it says:
reveal *to me all the good i have been asking for,*
but have been too lost in my own understanding to receive

surrender is an act of listening

it's me being quiet enough to hear
life whispering to me behind every
single moment:

i love you

what if

all this time

the answer was rest?

to everything i've been trying

to do
manifest
achieve
heal

what if,
just what if

what it's all been waiting on

is me
taking a break
letting go

and just
resting

what if i was already enough?

had done enough
had enough

and there was nothing else to do
but lay myself down

supinated, and receive

what if rest
was the missing piece?

for me, for us
for life

would i find it cruel that
i held it in my hand

all this time

and never looked at it?

when it finally happens

it's still hard to believe

(even though now is filled with
a ridiculous amount of
evidence)

that when you finally feel
enough and lovable

life bends over backwards

and sideways
and forwards

to prove that you
are, indeed

correct

if what i left behind

did not make me feel
more like myself

i won't be back for it

i've fucked men who didn't belong to me

it always seemed ok in the moment
but it never was afterwards

i've lied about who i am

what i have done
what i haven't done

to appear more likable
and more deserving of belonging
to people i wanted to impress

i've taken risks
and gotten burned for them

i've bared my heart to some men
who showed me many times before doing so
that this wasn't going to be a safe thing to do

i've made dumb financial decisions

lost money
not been able to pay my bills

i've hidden things about me

in order to have sex, and in order to
get in rooms where i believed my presence there would make
me more money

i've made some nasty choices
i've not always done the "right" thing

i guess what i'm trying to say here is
i've made mistakes

like you have

and like you

i'm still lovable
and loved

none of that diminishes this
none of that rejects this

it remains true

sometimes
we all need a reminder of this:
that we make mistakes

and love does not leave us,
even then

imagine, an alarm clock

that wakes you up every morning

not with loud discombobulating rings,
but with a softest of touch,
a slightest of whisper to:

wake up, joy is coming

i have traveled on my own titanic

and didn't sink

why is there no movie made about me?

is it because you are waiting to eat your popcorn
in front of screens that show only tragic ends?

not here

you will find me very much alive

even after aids
and kidney failure
and expectations lost

i still float

and when the credits roll
at the end of my story

they will say

starring....

the man who discovered anyone who uses
his own love as a life raft

cannot sink

the most underrated superfood

is an honest life.

a life where our being ambles
unsuppressed, unhidden,
without lies or pretending or editing.

this kind of life nourishes our cells better
than any green juice ever could.

we are made more beautiful by becoming
more truthful.

made more well not just by
focusing on what we eat,

but also by making sure we carry no secrets
that are eating at us.

i have bloomed in ways

there is no language for

there are parts of me that now know joy
that i never knew were previously starving for it

i am well nourished

i have stretched towards the sun
and received it

held it in my cells
fed off of it until i was full

i have dug my roots
in this soil and found water

drowned every dehydrated part
of my heart with it's unlimited flow

i am unfolded, and relaxed
surrendered

here

standing whole and beautiful
like i was meant to be

oh what a miraculous thing
it is what happens
when we have been

replanted
in love

guns in the hands of 18 yo boys (mostly white)

who have not been yet made to know

that lovable who is they are
loved is what they are
love is all we are

will take

everything
away

in playgrounds
and classrooms
and grocery stores
and church pews

from those still trying to remember
this for themselves

guns in the hands of those of us who have been made to lose
the memory of love

will steal this memory from others

a thousand fold

being made to forget
the love we are

is a violence devastating this country

one that never, ever
belonged in the hands of
children

i've known many men who have gone to war

but i haven't known any that returned from war,
alive.

even those that came home still breathing
were no longer living.

their eyes were vacant of the divine
and the breaths they did take were
short, shallow, afraid.

i've known many men who
came back home from war

but left their lights on the battlefields

uncles
grandads
coworkers
friends
lovers
neighbors

Jason
Thomas
Terry
Derrell
Claude
Terrell

they come back unable to shine,
unable to see their way through the dark,
unable to truly stand at ease,
unable to effectively aim and shoot
at the target of joy

even though it was standing still

they fought for what they were told was peace,
but were not told this fight would cost them their own

that they would have to offer their own ability
to know serenity as tribute

that it would be taken,
and may never return

what a real dishonor that was to them.

how we lie to those we say we love.

war does not birth
more life

in many ways, all that returns home from war
is the dead

but we are not told that sometimes,
the dead still breaths

that, we must find out on our own

and it is heartbreaking.

if i was ever to get a real tattoo

i think i want it to say

i am worthy of receiving it all

and i want it to be tattooed
on the tops of my feet
so that if i'm ever caught with
my head bowed down
(when it shouldn't be)

i will be reminded
to pick it up

and look forward

because good things
are coming
again

soon

nobody taught me

how to be a gay man

how to be

both masculine
and feminine

and some days,
something else entirely.

nobody taught me that

my sexuality has a power
a divinity
a purpose.

that the world is robbed of its own evolution

when i continue to not yet learn
that i must honor my hardness and my softness

that i must be nurturer, and protector
that i must be selfish, and selfless
that i must flow, and be ordered

be highly vocal, and deathly silent

that i must live in this balance

first for myself,
then for others

that i must be guided by these two energies within me

that i must stay silent at first
in any conflict
in any space
in any event

so i may hear which one most wants to lead in the moment

which one wants to most sit down for a second

which one wants to most expand

become more
bigger
louder

so that i am the best medicine in spaces,
instead of the best toxin

that my penis is pleasure,
but so is my ass

and that i am worthy of pleasure

that it wants to live all over my body
in the bedroom,

but also in my life

that when he says he loves me

i must listen to his words,
and the energy in his body

and if they are not the same

it is never true

and that i must only say yes to
building a life with

what is true

nobody taught me how to be a gay man

it has taken me multiple lifetimes
in this one life

to teach myself

no matter what phase it incurs

the moon remains the moon

whether it's full
or half
or sliver
or eclipsed

the moon remains itself

i must remember this
when my next phase comes

as surely it will
surely it must

that no matter what i incur
i still remain myself

i am still something
worthy of reverence
worthy of exploration

worthy of shifting the tides

my evening prayer

may i never again forget that
the one who deserves love most of all is me

in each and every time i feel i am most undeserving of it

may i never again believe that
there is a time and space and place that
does not hold love for me

may i never again forget that
i am able to stand solidly inside of and receive
my own belonging

may i never forget that
i can bring my dark,
my shadows,
my *he who shall not be nameds*

and name them
one by one

and place them in the light
so that they may be seen

may i remember that
no matter what it is that is
seen and named

it can only be
a part of me

and there is nothing, ever
about me

that is unlovable

may i never again commit
the sin of believing otherwise

no matter how many days i walk this earth

may the dementia of unlovability never again
take over my mind

relationships.

to whom it may concern:

letting them go because

they no longer nourish you,
no longer make you remember
the holiness of your own name,

no longer make you feel your soul
expanding within your own muscle tissues,

still hurts.

a lot sometimes.

i know no one tells you, but

leaving a place where
your roots run deep and entangled,
for newer, more fertilizing soil,
feels like new birth, and new death.

both come.
you will feel both.

your soul will ask you to keep walking forward
with both in your body.

don't you think it unfair

that you still call me?

that the phone rings,
and i see

your name

yet i still cannot stop my fingers
from pressing answer

that when i hear the sound of your voice
on the other end

my blood still quickens
my brain still smiles

even though our future has long
since been demolished

don't you find it an imbalance

how much control you have
over my heart?

even after it has long left
your hands

even after father time has shown us
it is not safe there

they say *all in love is fair*

so this is something other than love

yet, and still

i seem to want it

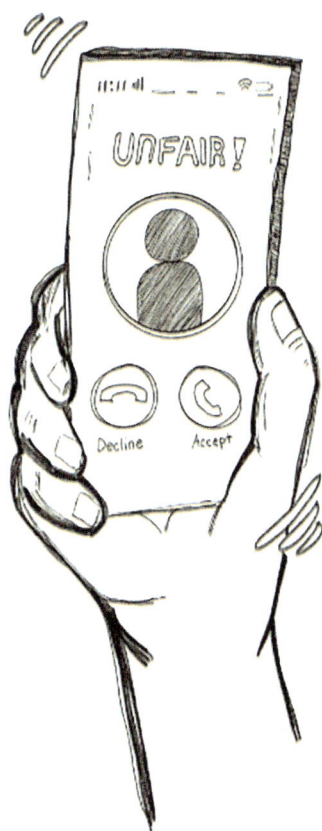

my favorite cologne

on a man

is peace

please,
wear this around me

it will turn me on

do you believe in reincarnation?

he asked me

of course
i say

for i have died a
thousand times
already

in this one lifetime

and found a thousand
more ways
to

come alive again

this me, here
is not the me that began

he is different, new
but still remembering
all the lives he had to
live and let die

to get to be here
now

able to experience love
with you

i want a man who

will walk towards me with
his heart open

his energy clear,
his body ready

like the rose unfolding
its pedals with the arrival
of the morning sun

i want to us
to meet each other,
and bloom

i did an adult thing today

maybe, the most adult thing
i've ever done

i got off my knees
unbowed my head
and

unfurled my hands
from prayer

retracted my shoulders
and opened my chest
and

admitted
to myself

that i am not ready for the love i said i wanted

that though worthy i am of someone else's love

ready to receive it
i am not

not to hold it
be a good steward of it
expand it

i cannot tell the courage it took
to speak these words aloud with my own tongue

that

i no longer want to be someone else's poison
but i have not yet learned how to be their medicine

because i am still learning how to be
my own

i love when he is a healing

that i do not
have to
bring to him

this is
its own
kind of

rest

this is
my own
kind of

answered prayer

i know that bonnie raitt said

"i can't make you love me, if you don't"

it was 1991
i was twelve

and i memorized and sang every word

in the shower
on my way to school
doing my homework
shooting free throws during basketball practice
running warm-up laps before a track meet

watching grandmomma pull her pound cake
out of the oven, and cut me a slice

i loved that song
breathed it

let it nourish the mitochondria
in my cells

and yet

i still tried anyway
(to make people love me when they don't)

for at least twenty more years.

it takes me so long
sometimes

to believe what has already been so
clearly spelled out for me

to integrate into my choices what already sings
itself in my bones

i left you to find

myself

i'm sorry if that hurt

but please know
i was hurting
even more

i have spent many years screaming

from the top
of my lungs

how adored i deserve to be!

how much those
who show up
in my life have
neglected this

withheld this

meanwhile

never adoring myself
enough to no longer choose

people, situations, places
that starve me of
love

what a ridiculous betrayal
i have been
to myself

i listen to words and bodies

both.

i need to hear both.

tell me you love me
with your mouth

and i will also listen to
your shoulders

do they rise and tighten
or relax and expand
when you say it?

tell me you're happy

and i will listen to your eyes

do they blind me with the shine of your soul?

or are they blank and darkened by
no comfort or hope?

tell me you are sure

and i will listen to your feet
as they hit the floor

do they make music with the earth
with light, but solid steps?

or are they heavy, clunking, overburden
with confusion and regret?

tell me you feel alive
and i will listen to your breath

do i hear the depth of the ocean in your exhale?

or the shallowness of
dreams deferred?

i want to listen to you in this beloved moment

but i will listen to all of you

the truth your body shares, and the lies
your mouth is trying to believe

i get hard when

i see him

soaking wet
drenched

and

doused in
his soul.

– *fetish*

i was quartz

breath of the white dragon

power, energy, clarity
healing, balance, creation

but you were no geologist

you just saw rocks
with pointy edges

and made your way
onwards

towards softer things

he wanted to devour me

to ravage
my body
on silk
sheets

like the lion
on a gazelle

so hungry
he said
he was

but

i let him
drink from
my soul
instead

deep cavernous gulps

til he
realized

just how much his hunger
was just

dehydration

more than anything

i wish you could see how much

i loved me

how much i delight
in me

how much pleasure i get from
my own being

i have tried to wear it on my sleeves,
sew it into the hems of my pants

place it on top of my head, cocked to the side
like my grandfathers grey hat

i wanted this to be seen

so you would know not
to ask me to stay

i wish you knew how much i loved me

so you didn't have to
hurt tonight

because i am not meant to stay
in places

where i am expected to love
me less

if i'm being honest

i'm horny
i'm hungry
i'm lonely
i want to be hugged
i want to be kissed on the back of my neck
i want to laugh until my sides hurt

i want to be emotionally soothed until
my sides are the only things that hurt on me

and i'd like all of these things
to be addressed at the same time

by the same person

how do you say

i want you, but
i *need me*

at the same time?

how do you say

you are everything my body
is screaming to taste

but me is everything my soul
has been screaming to eat

in the same breath?

how do you say

my plate is full of you
but my stomach is starved of me

it's GOODBYE isn't it?

GOODBYE is how you say it?

damn

i lived a lifetime knowing

loneliness is a space where i know that
my loved ones exist and
i hope that someone who will love me exists

but i cannot reach them, and
i am not being reached

but now, i know loneliness is falling asleep
in the bed after you do

not having your eyes look into my soul
as you turn over and put your hand on my chest
while i drift off to sleep with the shape of your goatee

as my last conscious image

loneliness now is me knowing
that my loved ones exists,
and someone who loves me exists,
and that he is sleeping first, right next to me,

while i have to wait just a few more hours
to be truly seen again, by him

i so much prefer this kind of loneliness

thank you for bringing it to me

once i welcome a man home

into my heart

two things usually happen

he learns
though it looks
like any ole regular
neighborhood shanty

it's bigger
on the inside

and i learn
though small
and filled to every
corner, already

home can
always hold
more love

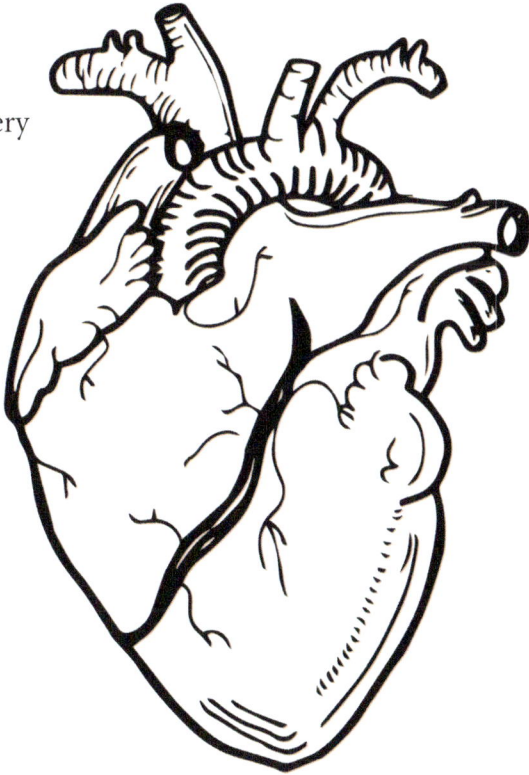

i have not always been the best lover

i have withheld affection
attention
nourishment

i have left needs unmet
and love languages
unspoken

i have not been faithful
not been truthful
not been full of hope, or joy
or anything else someone needs
to feel being with me
is home

i have had to come to terms
with the fact
that sometimes,

when there was no love left
in your heart for me

it was because of me

i left the door open for it
to walk out

is this about me?

he asked, while reading a poem
i've written about a man
i love that

i cannot have

he's married

and his wife is a soul
so beautiful it
belongs in a museum

just looking at her makes
me feel lighter, more in awe

and as much as i want love
i don't think i want the kind that
comes from destroying another's

i want the love that comes to me with no
broken shards attached

no places that will cut my hand
when i reach for it

no pain that will eventually get sewn into my own back while
i'm sleeping

i want a love that comes to me clean

so, *no*, i tell him

it is not about you

but i have lied

it is
it always is

he is my greatest yearning

the thought of him accompanies
my every inhale

the way his black skin reminds me of coffee
the way his muscles seem to move underneath his skin like
snakes, the way his heart, his heart never seems to shrink

the way his voice sounds like mountains, moving closer
together, so they may better hear one another

but i do not want to have him
like this

i do not want to have him
when having him comes with regret

but this, too, is a lie

it is a dream that i have when i sleep
that if the day ever came when i
would have to make the choice

between having him dirty,

or not having him at all

i would choose to not have him at all

knowing that i could sleep better at night
having done the "right" thing
and there was no one who's life would end
by me trying to start another chapter of my own

but, i already do not sleep better at night

for i dream of a life with him with my eyes wide open

wanting something you can have
but shouldn't

is a wound

that i am still trying to learn how
to turn into wisdom

with this needle

made from
all the honey
of his love

i pull the remaining
threads of you

from my skin

that used to tell me
i don't deserve

better

please take me off the shelf

brush me
off, and

turn me
over

check my
expiration date

and decide
too much time
has past

for you

to

keep

waiting

to

taste

me

— *dating while horny*

remember when you

asked me
what i'd be

if i could be
anything i wanted
to be?

and i said *whole*

and then
you left me?

i understand
now

thank you.

they say finding love

is *finding someone better than*
spending time alone

i guess

but

sometimes i think it's finding someone who
makes me feel like the spaces i
discover in myself
when there's no one else around
trying to make me be
something, someone else

i think love is me
finding myself

then finding someone who
reminds me that

this, alone
is enough

walk towards me, brother

not away
not on the side

let your movements towards me always
be in the direction of merging

i do not bite,
outside of the bedroom

your heart and skin
are safe with me

there are no wounds here,
only medicine

move in closer

we have oneness to do

what i wish for you:

that you are understood
that you are seen

that what is seen and understood
is accepted, and valued

even celebrated

that you are made to know that
you deserve to be held, deserve to be heard

deserve to have your wounds tucked in at night
and kissed softly to sleep

that you never have to ask
more than twice

for what you need
what you want, what you crave

never have to ask for a compliment

or affection
or time

but receive them freely, frequently

this is my wish for you

all the love that you
withheld from me

you left because

i was a black
sun

rare, massive

with worlds still needing my
gravitational pull

you

failed astrology

thought i was
just a star needing
to hurry up

and die out

when i love a man

he gets all my heart
right away

i do not know how to show up
any other way
but fully

this has rocked me to
my core
at times

i have been burnt
because of this

but, this has also
healed me

i have known deeper levels of receiving,
greater levels of gratitude, wider levels of intimacy

every time i break
i receive more,
better

it's a fair trade
i think

willing to be broken

if that breaking
opens me up to

more

i am a man
who shows up with
all of his heart
willing to break

so that he can break
in the direction of better

when i think of all that time

i spent with you

i can't help but smile

not because those days
were filled with honey
or warm sunlight

or even slight amusement

i smile because
those days are
soaked, and oozing
with wisdom

of what no longer works for me
of what no longer turns the light on
behind my eyes

of what no longer makes me feel alive

valuable lessons
given, and learned, and

now applied

thank god for those days

i know what better is now
because i have lived what it
is not

and for that, i smile

because of you

i no longer

choose to be where better does not dwell

my mother is a thing

that holds my hand
by the bedside where i am trying
not to take my last breath

a thing that withdraws her last amount of savings
so that i may have that surgery i need

a thing that rocks me in it's arms when i have fallen
to the floor at 35 and cannot stand

both from the illness, and from the shame

my mother is a thing that is there
when even most of me is not
cannot

a thing that holds steady when i am trying to find a
way out of no way

but have no more strength
to take even one more step

my mother is a thing that became my legs
and walked me through the doorway of hope

a thing that speaks possibility over my cells
to defend me against the valley of the shadow of
death

a thing that sewed *persevere* into the joints of my
spine

with needles of prayer and tears
and the spiritual unwillingness
to let dying be her last memory of me

my mother is not a perfect thing,
but she is a thing that gave me life
more than once

thank god for her

so many think i put this life together on my own

they see my walk and talk
and believe i wove this out of
my own hands

with my own thread
in my own time

but

my life is a tapestry of
ancient prayers

said in closets, and

break rooms, and hospitals,
and wooden pews, and

around kitchen tables, and in open fields,
and in office cubicles, and
softly in dark corners

prayers stitched together by

tears, and
hope and
forgiveness, and

unwavering longings to step
through doors with doorknobs

that had never turned to open

uttered by grandparents, and
parents, and nurses, and
teachers, and lovers, and
friends, and

spirits looking on from
realms i cannot yet go

my life was built by folded hands

and bended knees
and sore feet
and bent backs
and broken hearts
and unbreakable spirits

of those seen and unseen
who love me

(if even for just
a few moments)

i walk on these prayers daily

like eggshells, sometimes
cobblestones, on others

nevertheless aware

that i walk now on sacred ground
because it has been blessed for my arrival

by those who wished for me
better

fulfillment is

when a lover tells me

i make them feel
more like themselves

because i just do not think there is anything better to do in
this life

than to make someone feel
more like themselves

what a delicious accomplishment
of my purpose here

what a glorious invitation to
keep on living

and try to discover if there is something
yet still out there
better than this

self–healing.

can i be me?

can i sit in the seat of my own authenticity,
and drive life from here?

can i steer unedited
unsuppressed
unhidden

unabashed?

can i let my
deepest yearnings be my compass?

can my quirkiness be the music
i listen to on the radio to
keep my eyes awake long enough
to make it to the next stop?

instead of my ten and my two
can i place my hands on my sensitivity
and my sexuality

and make the right turns?

and if i do
will i arrive where i
think i'm headed?

will i get there in time
with all my senses in order
and no wrinkles or stains on the
dreams i put on to wear

for this ride?

can my truth
really be the road?

will there be enough places to stop
along it when i need a few moments
to rest my eyes
stretch my legs
learn from my mistakes?

i am ashamed to reveal how much life i've spent trying so
studiously to
answer this question

knowing what the real answer is
already

and i am saddened to reveal that most of my life
i have answered

the wrong answer

"no"

i am many things

and i am not
many things

but mainly, i am
myself

and i am not
all the messages

i've been trying
to eat

that said what i am
is not enough

he asked me if i believed

that other worlds exist

yes, i told him

for i walk in and out of
different versions of me

every day

and within each version
the world is different

more loving,
less loving

more safe,
less safe

in some worlds i laugh more,
in others less

i know different worlds exists,
i say

because i have lived within
different versions of me

and i continue to try to figure out which of my
versions will allow me to land in the world that is
truly my home

the one where i am more alive,
more like myself

instead of less

how can you be

so loving
towards people?

she
asked me

hugs and sunsets
and scar tissue fell
out of my lips
as i responded

because
i have been

unloved

so, i decided
long ago

that i have lived

unloved enough
for all of us

i was taught to hate

the feminine in me

the parts that wanted to
be soft, tread gently
feel things deeply
be led by the heart

the parts that liked my little pony's over gi joe
volleyball over football
listening over talking

i was made to feel shame for
the way my wrist naturally
found it's way into a resting limp

the way my heart stayed on my sleeve
like it was sewn there with purpose

to recoil at the sound of my own voice
played back to me on recording devices

too high pitched
too at home in softness
and trust

too much like a girl, they said
meaning, too weak
too different

too unlovable

and so i did

i recoiled
i shamed
i unloved

those parts

tried to cut and burn and bury

the she in me

thinking that only the he
was enough

only the he
would + could belong
would + could be loved
would + could be safe in this world

there are days like today
where my arms are not enough to
carry the weight of grieving i have
for this

i was made to leave myself

i do not know a greater punishment
suffering, tragedy

than to leave home from what you are
believing somewhere else carries
more welcome

more safety
more joy

i am just now learning how safe it is
lovable it is, joyful it is

holy it is

to make my way back home
to her

she belongs to me

i am he, and she

and this wholeness
is home

oh how unwell i have been
without it

me is a thing

i am still

learning
how to

love

i am tearing down a home

where the walls
are made of fear,

the floor is made
from imported shame,

the windows are caked
in overwhelm,

the kitchen bakes only
inadequacy, served hot
and in too much amounts,

the roofs been
artistically crafted
in illness,

the mortgage is always
too much, way, way too much.

i am tearing down my life

moving to another one
i'd love to come home to

in a better neighborhood

with a healthier, happier
foundation

i have been scared to let the darkest parts of me see the light

in the truest, most realest way,

i have been terrified that if i let my darkness out to play in the
sun,
it will eat everything

the foliage,
the livestock,
the approval
the love

and leave nothing behind itself but death

it's the death that i'm afraid of

death of this life that i know
that my brain so assuredly convinces me will come

funny, if i'm being totally
honest

i'm afraid of the arrival of a death that i secretly pray would
come

because as much as i love life,
i do not love this life

of hiding
things

so hard

that are trying so hard

to be seen.

i am so scared of death
and so tired of shadows

and so curious about
playing in the light
fully seen

last night, i dreamt

that my future self called
my cell phone

and when i picked up,
all he said was:

be softer with us

i do not want to hold so tightly to things

that i forget to hold
onto myself

i have done this in the past

held to a thing
and let go of myself

it seemed like such
the right thing to do
at the time

but it never was

never is

never will be

this is the danger in
not letting go

we may keep what we struggle so mightily not to lose

but we lose
what we forget
we really wanted

our own peace

happiness
sense of self

may i remember now
that it is safe to let go

may it be shown to me
in doing so that

what i release
was never more important
than what stays here

within me

i spent my whole life

drinking the poison
you gave me

and calling it water

pouring it on my plants

and the life that surrounded
my home

blind to the fact they
had all been

long dead

– *toxic narratives*

i have struggled mightily over the years to find my own existence's elevator pitch

one word to let you know all of what i am

poet
psychic
gay
black
man
introvert
empath

but i have not
cannot

maybe because

me
just doesn't feel enough
(though it is)

and *everything feels too much*
(though it isn't)

i am both *me,*
and *everything*

and *part of you,* too

and so many other things that

added up together
let you know that
what i am is a thing

that is loved
and lovable

and right here
still having to remember
how true all of this is

i am magic

the magic

i am more
magic than

you've ever seen

the kind that makes
miracles, and
elixirs, and

new worlds,
and old wounds
heal

i am magic
the magic

because i am
finally loved

by my own self

you sound like
a girl

she said

to my five year old body
in giggles

that looped in the air

then nosedived
like kamikazes on
the landscape of my psyche

leaving the part of me

dead

that still believed

nothing was
wrong with me

– *trauma*

i wish my life to taste of

delicious.

that my living sticks to the roof of my mouth like
fresh almond butter

that my to-do list is marinated in honey, leaving
the events of my days staining my memories with something
that tastes

like pleasure

i wish my mornings to feel like
the light that pours through my bedroom
windows on sunday mornings

lazy, stretched out, and
pooled lightly at the bottom hem
of my sheets

i wish my afternoons to smell of rest,
of drinking hot tea in terrycloth robes,
of champagne brunches with best friends,
of staring out of large-paned windows
towards vast, and sweeping, and
picturesque terrains

i wish my evenings to flavor themselves
with freshly watered flowers, and
texts from my favorite him that say
*"i thought of you all day, and
i cannot wait to do it again tomorrow"*

i wish my midnights to feel of
walks on the beach when the dolphins
are playing in the waves, and

sex with a him who sees not just
the shape of my abs, but also
the shape of my light

i want myself a scrumptious life

so that on my last day of it, i shall
get up from the table fully satisfied,
not able to take one more bite

but totally, whole-heartedly,

still wanting to

i wish there was a way to audibly hear my heart

like through a megaphone

or a loud chanting crowd in a stadium
or a baby's scream from the crib
or you talking and chewing too loudly
in this movie theater
while i'm trying to watch this film

some audible vibration
that rings in my ears
so i couldn't ignore when it

told me the loneliness that
ate my heart

could've been well fed, instead
by spending more time by the ocean

and writing with the windows open

and laughing way too long and hard
at reruns of family guy

i think maybe that way

i wouldn't have spent so much time
feeling alone

and more time actually being

accompanied by
my own joy

funny, how what we think we need

is for parts of ourself to be + do
more than they are

in order to be happy sooner

i think that's a part of loneliness, too -
not connecting to the knowing that

what i am and
how i naturally work

is already enough

that being different
won't fix it

or make me happy

but learning how to
accept and be with it

will

i'd like to save myself

from myself

not by running away from

but by knocking on
my own front door

and opening it

and welcoming myself in

and sitting down in
the living room and serving myself tea

and talking with myself about

all the places it hurts
and how tired i've been

and then lying my head down in my own lap
to take a deep rest while myself strokes
my hair

and hums

melodically singing
that i'll be ok here

that i'll always be
ok here

that i've always been
ok

here

what i really want

is to love me back
into myself

my soul has been trying

to get me to write the same poem
my entire life

on white lined-paper
on school text books
on sticky notes
on love letters
on business contracts
on legal documents
on to-do lists
on the hearts of the men i've desired

it begins with
there is

and ends with
nothing wrong with me

last year, i learned to rest

i learned to
release and let things go

until i am light enough to hear
the sound of myself living again

i learned to
remember to say no,

(not just to what i don't want to do,
but to whatever was *good* when what
i really yearned for is what is *delicious*)

i learned that
being busy isn't a badge of honor

but a disease we wear on the lapels of
our suit jackets hoping
someone will see it and say:

*that's a mighty fine badge you got there,
must mean you finally belong here,
you're finally enough here*

and that these words would be the elixir that makes
us forget just how much pain we're in
(they aren't)

i learned that
no matter how many times
my mind says something can't wait,

it always can
(especially social media)

i learned that
sleep is both a medicine, and a portal

where i meet more of my
true self, and bring more of my
true self's wisdom back home with me
when i awake (if i do it enough)

i learned that
our culture has taught us to sometimes
spell success two different ways:
b u r n o u t and *e x h a u s t i o n*

i learned that
leisure is my liberation

that to slow down and
lay in the grass and
let the sun play on my skin
without a phone in my hand
or a to-do list in my head
is my ancestors answered prayer for me

i learned that
the hustle and grind culture is
violence (against myself)

and another form of slavery
that i can choose this time
whether to participate in, or not

(i choose not)

i learned that achievements mean
nothing if i'm too tired to enjoy them

i learned that my cell phone + tv don't
belong in my bedroom

or my lap in the car,
or at the beginning of my day

because these spaces belong to peace,
instead of to what strives to take my peace away

i learned that
i owe my nervous system the kind of life
it wants to be alive in

that it's been through enough, already

and never, ever needed to earn the ease and serenity that feeds
it in the first place

i learned that
being well-rested is unpopular
but so is happiness

(*that i prefer the unpopular path*)

sissy

used to burn my skin like napalm

used to break my bones like all the words that
"would never hurt me"

used to destroy the soul in my soft tissues like a vat
of hydrofluoric acid

they said it to me to make me feel that a black boy
with a limp wrist and an alto voice didn't belong
here

not just in this schoolyard blacktop
not just in this neighborhood
not just in this race, this gender, this animal skin

but in this universe
this galaxy

this reality

sissy
is the identity i had to reclaim to divest myself from
unworthiness, unlovability, unbelonging

to make *oversensitive, soft, not a man like us* my
sacred home

despite the seductive and sticky tendrils of
masculinity and approval calling me to root my
light down into suppression and obedience.

it's funny that the word we have for this kind of life is

"*queer*": different, weird, not like the rest

i think i am just unboxed, unwilling to settle,
no longer able to press through life
unhappy, unfulfilled

unmyself

isn't it funny how we have made cutting parts of
ourselves off, and the absence of wholeness and joy,
the norm

and tried so hard to convince everyone that this is ok?

it is not

and if i have to be a *sissy* to remind us,
with whatever limp in my wrist
whatever twist in my walk
whatever softness in my talk

that exists as i mosey
queerly on down the road,

i shall, i shall, forevermore

somewhere there is

stardust in these cells

that still
remembers

it is ok
to let the lights go out

because
we are the light

we are
the reason

i must find it,
the stardust

it must help
me remember

it must

i must

i wish

people would just leave me alone

i say to the air

about
all the people
i become

when i feel i'm not enough

lovable is

these scars on my neck,
this back fat,
this trembling voice as
i speak up for what i need.

lovable is
this health status,
this zero bank account balance,
this ugly truth,

these embarrassing moments,
these failures,
these wins.

lovable is everything
i am, and
am trying not to be.

the ugly,
the beautiful,

the me.

the whole me.
unconditionally.

i will forever see lovable
when i look in the mirror.

even when i forget

when i heard the nurse say hiv+

what i heard was

poisoned
unwanted
unwantable

not worthy to be seen in public

not possible to exist just as i am,
and be loved at the same time

what i heard was

there is something wrong with me
so my belonging is no longer safe

no longer assured
because there is

what i heard was

who will love you now, that
you are no longer enough,
no longer lovable

and never will be again?

what i heard was

your body is gross
how dare it take up space here

what i heard was

you are alone now
so, so, so alone

isn't it funny (and sad)

what we hear in the air with our ears

when they have not yet been taught

how to attune themselves to
the softer and truer sounds

of unconditional love?

i am tired of

waiting
at the door

pulling back the
curtains

peering and
straining my eyes

to see

if maybe
just maybe

that's me there
in the distance

making my way
back home

to myself.

wherever i am

is a healing atmosphere

because i am willing to be myself
unedited, unhidden

in world that tells
me, you, us
that *this alone is unsafe,*
unwelcomed, unworthy

my authenticity is an elixir
because it dares to publicly say,

no, this is a lie

black seed oil

green juice
apple cider vinegar
sea moss
alkaline water
plant-based meals
vitamins and herbs

are not enough
to be optimally well

we must also eat our own acceptance

ingest our own appreciation
and respect and trust

we must learn how to feed ourselves
daily

what we really need

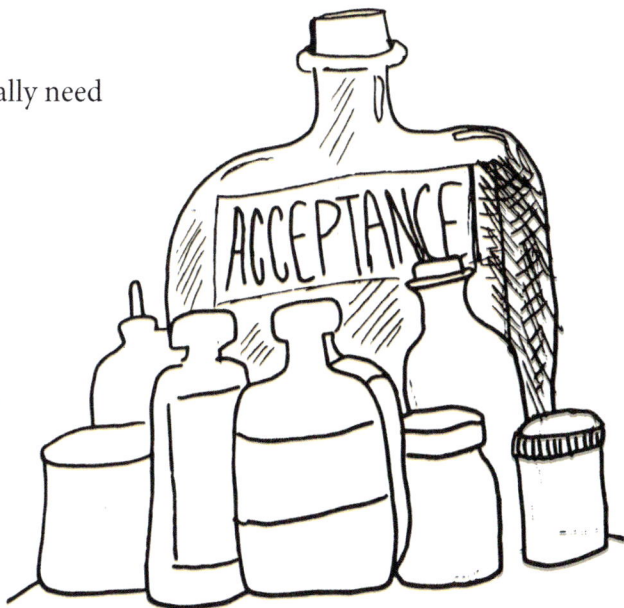

i have waited so long to become

the one who is seen

the one who is open
who radiates
who steps out of shadows
and glows

the one who is unhidden

i spent years telling myself that the shadows
were the safest place

that dark was the best nourishment
the most nutritious dwelling

i packed away all my most sacred and raw
parts there, tucked them under the darkest soil
whispered them sweet secrets to be ridden
by the whirling shadows

but i see now how i've lied to myself

light is so much more nutritious
to live in

being seen is so much more delicious
a home

he surrendered

he let go of needing them to be different
he let go of needing to be different himself

and accepted who they are
what he is

now, as is

he let go of needing them to love him
he let go of needing to love them up close

and embraced the pain of loving them
from a distance, welcomed the pain of
realizing if this isn't meant to be, not his highest good, not his
most authentic fulfillment

then it's better left over there

he let go of needing them in order to be ok,
in order to be happy, in order to be enough

and yielded to the idea that his okness
is not conditional

nor his happiness,
nor his enoughness

he just surrendered, let go

and fell

and then,
his worthiness caught him

it was in the catching
that he healed

it is always in the being caught by
our own worthiness
that we heal

but first, we must fall

and to fall,
we must let go

of everything we have our hands wrapped
around that's making us forget

that falling back
into our worthiness

is more than safe

it's medicine

my body.

my body is where god dwells

it's the home of god,
you might say

which means my body is heaven

(cause that's the only place god
calls home)

but i have spent eternity thinking
it was

where not enoughness resides
where ugliness answers the door
where shame chimes her chippy little voice when you press
the doorbell

where failure cuts the grass and trims the bushes
where exhaustion has amazon deliver her packages

all this time i thought this was hell

and have embarrassingly been looking for god
elsewhere

a letter from my body to me:

promise me

you will learn to truly see me
no matter how beautiful i am

no matter how much it hurts that you
thought i wasn't, for so long

promise me

you will truly see
what's actually here

waiting

to be finally
recognized

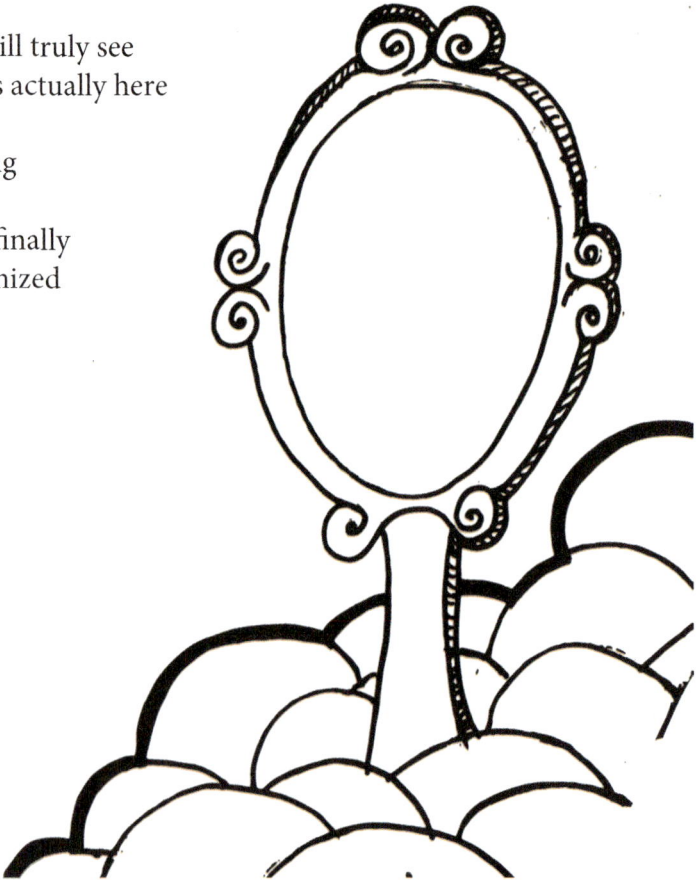

"your kidneys have failed"

doctors have such a violent way
of speaking

me, i think they're just
sleeping

dreaming of days when i'll know how
to take better care of myself

not by eating better, per se
but by better tending to
what's been eating at me

by not letting days go by (again)
without dancing

without singing

without making silly, nonsensical jokes
about how *big butts don't lie*

without gazing out of the window until the next
poem comes

without tending to what's in my heart before
i tend to what's in my inbox

without saying *no* more until
i can clearly hear my *yes*

without feeling more free

feeling more joy

feeling more like me

i think they will wake up again one day

you see, anyone who lives in bondage will sleep
so that they can dream of freedom

my kidneys have not failed

they are simply trying to temporarily escape
a life they were not built for

i will wake them again

once i have become a more delicious life
than their wildest dreams

i will wake them again

i promise

if i can laugh today

i must

if i can dance today
i must

if i can write today
i must

if i can hear my best friend's voice
i must

if i can drink hot ginger tea,
and eat blueberries,
and soak in a hot bath
with jazz softly playing on
the surround sound speakers
i must

i will
i must

for who knows if there will be a tomorrow
for me

my health is on borrowed
diminishing time
they say

so today, i must
know joy

every monday, wednesday, friday

i let a machine suck out my soul

clean it

and try and give it back to me

but it has been touched by foreign hands
who do not love it

only process and clean it

i wonder if they knew how clean it would be
if when they took it from me

they sang to it

they fed it blueberries
and red gummy bears
in small, white porcelain bowls

they walked it by the ocean and
let it watch the waves roll over
scattering sand onto its toes

they let it watch my mother
take her famous sweet potato pie
out of the oven
and say she could've done better

(though there is no better for perfect)

they wrapped it in sweatpants and
fuzzy blankets and handed it
a cup of hibiscus tea

they let it put on skinny jeans and v-neck shirts
and parade in front of dark-skinned men who's
muscles cannot be unseen

they let it listen to my best friend's laughter
on a loop playing over loud speakers

i wonder how pristine the essence of
my soul would be, then
as it made its way back
through that dialysis machine

down through the tubes and needles
back home into the veins of my arm

how clean and able it
would be to keep me alive

we try so hard to make things sterile
and fail so terribly

because we often forget to
wash them first

in love

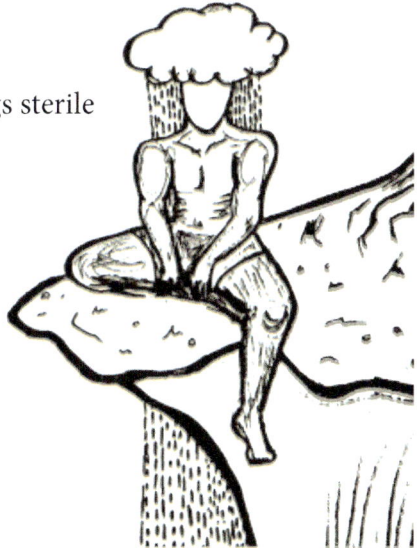

my body is a museum

of natural disasters

i am just now
learning

to accept

how beautiful
that is

i shall find my way again

to trails weaving
down mountainsides

to fires burning
on campgrounds

to kayaks floating lazily
down rivers

to sweat dripping off chests
on gymnasium floors

to swimming nude
in oceans

to booking flights at the whim

i shall find my way again

disease will not be
my last destination

i will arrive back home to well
and happy

a forgiveness letter to my body:

i'm sorry i'm sorry i'm sorry i'm sorry i'm sorry
i'm sorry i'm sorry i'm sorry i'm sorry i'm sorry
i'm sorry i'm sorry i'm sorry i'm sorry i'm sorry
i'm sorry i'm sorry i'm sorry i'm sorry i'm sorry
i'm sorry i'm sorry i'm sorry i'm sorry i'm sorry
i'm sorry i'm sorry i'm sorry i'm sorry i'm sorry
i'm sorry i'm sorry i'm sorry i'm sorry i'm sorry
i'm sorry i'm sorry i'm sorry i'm sorry i'm sorry
i'm sorry i'm sorry i'm sorry i'm sorry i'm sorry
i'm sorry i'm sorry i'm sorry i'm sorry i'm sorry
i'm sorry i'm sorry i'm sorry i'm sorry i'm sorry
i'm sorry i'm sorry i'm sorry i'm sorry i'm sorry
i'm sorry i'm sorry i'm sorry i'm sorry i'm sorry
i'm sorry i'm sorry i'm sorry i'm sorry i'm sorry
i'm sorry i'm sorry i'm sorry i'm sorry i'm sorry
i'm sorry i'm sorry i'm sorry i'm sorry i'm sorry
i'm sorry i'm sorry i'm sorry i'm sorry i'm sorry
i'm sorry i'm sorry i'm sorry i'm sorry i'm sorry
i'm sorry i'm sorry i'm sorry i'm sorry i'm sorry
i'm sorry i'm sorry i'm sorry i'm sorry i'm sorry

i'm sorry
i'm sorry
i'm sorry
i'm sorry
i'm sorry
i'm sorry
i'm sorry
i'm sorry
i'm sorry
i'm sorry

i'm sorry
i'm sorry
i'm sorry
i'm sorry

for taking so long to see
just how fucking worthy you are

of my own love

i have starved you of it,
and there is no excuse

but i promise

you will be well fed
from here on

i'm in love with the color of my skin

the copper brown tones of it
the way it darkens
in the sun

the way sometimes when i catch myself
at the right angle in the mirror

i look like the color

of safety
and mysticism

and something to toil
and plant beautiful things in

i laugh sometimes

at how i was taught something
this beautiful

was not

and then i laugh again

at how stunning the contrast is between
the brown of my skin

and the white of my
laughing teeth

they say my scars

are evidence that i lived

that i survived
through something

and now have triumph etched
on my skin

that they are cosmic celebrations

something to frame, if i could
and show off proudly to all those
who visit my home

they say my scars mean *i won*

but for me,

they are evidence of
something else entirely

when i catch a glimpse of them
in a mirror, or on the beach when the
sun dances itself lightly across their raised
topography

i do not see triumph,
but betrayal

not by the scar itself,
for it is a sacred thing

but by myself

see, every scar i have on my body
has come at the end of a time where i
didn't listen

to myself

where i placed someone else's
voice, judgment, opinion

as the authority
over that of my own soul

i do not own a scar that was not gifted to me
from betrayal

whether they are the ones on
my chest or groin from
catheter surgeries

or the ones scaling the entire range of
my right arm from
fistula surgeries

or the one camping out
across the center of my knee

that came to visit after i didn't listen
to my body screaming to be stretched out
before running hurdles at a
track meet

they each speak of what happens
when i ignore myself

of what happens when i
forget that no one else knows, or
will know what's best for me

better than the wisdom
that sits solidly in my own gut

my scars are not witnesses of battles won,
but daily reminders of lessons learned

i do not have scars
i have tattoos

and every single one of them says

remember to trust yourself,
above all else

i woke up this morning and felt good about my body

do you know what that feels like?

to feel good about a body you used to hate?

to look on scars riding across the crevices of your limbs, and
not see flaw, but beauty?

to spot fat pooling in areas where
it wasn't preferred, and

not see shame
but acceptance?

to spy gaps and yellowing in teeth and
not see something to fix,

but something to flaunt?

to see aging changes that weren't asked for,
but welcome them all the same?

to glimpse stretch marks and not feel disgust,
but growth?

i can search a thousand dictionaries
and visit a million libraries

and never find the right descriptive words
that would filter through your ears

and settle behind
the muscles in your chest
in the expansive way that this
deserves to be known

but i can say this

and hope it is enough
to make you understand

this, too, is something
you should know

we all should know

we are all worthy
of knowing

it feels like
coming alive

at some point

me and god need to
have a long talk
about dialysis

and by long i mean
me, just asking

WHY?

ten million times
in a row

i was listening to a podcast the other day

and the host had a guest
on who was dealing with cancer

and she asked him:
"what does chemo feel like?"

"like losing hope"
"like millions of little pins poking holes in your dreams"
"like wishing life was anything but this"

and as i listened
to their response

i realized

nobody has ever asked me:

what does dialysis feel like?

what does four and a half hours of your day,
three times a week,

feel like?

what does not being able to ever sleep in on
mondays, wednesdays, or fridays
because your chair time is 6:30 am

feel like?

what does being pricked by a needle deeper and
wider than any tear you have ever mustered for yourself

feel like?

what does developing a close relationship with the
nurse who puts you on the machine each time only
to have them leave for another job, a year later,
because they realized this is no longer what they
want to do, leaving you realizing you don't have
that same luxury

feel like?

what does sitting in a chair
that is not located in your home
not being able to move or get up
while you watch your life force drain out of you
through a tube, and return to you again through
another tube

feel like?

what does getting to know your dialysis seat
neighbors - how they got sick, what their favorite tv
show is, how their wife is dealing with them now
being disabled, what their favorite recipe for fried
chicken is, how their kids are doing so much better
in school now since they got that tutor, how they

used to be a naval officer, how excited they are to
finally be on the transplant list,

only to have them die a few months later,
and you are not given their address to send flowers,
or the time and date of their funeral to attend,

feel like?

what does hearing susan say "*hey jerome, honey!*"
every morning for four years, as you pass her
dialysis chair on your way to your own, and then
coming in one friday excited to tell her how much
her greeting meant to you all these years, only to
see her chair empty,

not because she was in the hospital,
or had gotten a new kidney,
or a had decided to skip treatment that day

but because she was no longer able to say
"*hey jerome, honey!,*" or anything else,
to anyone else, ever again

feel like?

what does frequent cramps, worse than any pain
you've had in all the surgeries you've had, that no
banana can ease, no gatorade can relieve, and that
always seem to hit once you've reached home,
alone, and no one else is around, or capable to help
you relieve them, so you scream for an hour into
thin, alone air

feel like?

maybe, i'll tell them

it, too, feels like

"losing hope"
"like millions of little pins poking holes in your dreams"
"like wishing life was anything but this"

or maybe,
i'll tell them the truth

it feels like

gratitude

for the opportunity a clunky machine is giving me
to see one more day of living

gratitude

for the unasked for, but highly welcomed, chance to
figure out how much love and joy a person can fit
into three hours of day - all the waking hours i can
muster after treatment is finished

gratitude

for awakening me to how short life really is

and how little time we really have to say *i love you*
to the ones we love, to eat our favorite dish one
more time (mom's spaghetti), to take the risk to
finally, finally, be happy, and to love our one, wild
and unique self, illness and all

gratitude

for teaching me though my life may be
painful and exhausting, it's still worth waking up to

still worth exploring
still worth tasting
still worth making plans for

still worth living

gratitude.

yes, i think this is what i'd really say,
if they had ever asked me

there is a dialysis catheter in my right leg

it is white
with blue and red caps

it attaches itself into my right thigh
and journeys itself through an artery
all the way to my heart
where it plants its roots

to help me survive

i wish i knew how to make this sexier

how to say it in a way that made you want me

want to buy satin sheets and place me on them
in the middle of the night with white candles and
music and chocolate-covered fruits at the ready
in case you couldn't resist letting yourself do
all manner of things to me that would
make you smile

and sweat

and explore the very edges of your desire
on my body

especially my right leg

who at times i know feels starved for
that kind of adoration

but i am left only knowing how to say this
in a way that is true

it is true

and i am not sure if it is sexy to you
or not

but i am trying to make it beautiful
to me

because, though i do not want it

i still need it

and i think i believe the key
to becoming something that is sexy

is to become something that learns how to make
whatever is needed and true something
i am no longer ashamed of

q: what does it mean to be hiv+?

a: it means that i must figure out how to remember
that i am alive, in a world of everyone who has forgotten.

it means that i must remind myself that air still
figures out how to make it's way through my lungs,
that my legs still figure out every evening around 6 pm
how to dance in zumba class, that my heart
(though tired at times) still figures out how to beat
to the drumbeat of appreciation for the sight of
roses and sing along with the melody of forgiveness
for all the ways i wished i knew how to treat myself
better when i was younger

it means that my brain still figures out what bills to
pay on time, which emails to put on read,
which scheduled appointments can actually be
rescheduled, which affirmations will make me feel
most safe when i walk through the doorway of a
doctor's office, which colors to put on my walls and
crystals to place on my shelves so that i feel every
time i cross over the threshold of my front door that
my home is a holy retreat center from fear

whilst everyone else is figuring out a cornucopia of
ways to remind themselves that i am dying

it means that i must remember to figure out how to
remember that i am still worthy of love, worthy of
affection, worthy of being ravaged wildly, worthy
of eating gummy bears and mom's spaghetti and thai

180

food and nachos and dessert, even though they tell
me none of this will inspire my t-cells to multiply

it means i must figure out how to remember i am
still worthy of the experience of pleasure finding it's
way into my skin, and over the terror in my tissues,
down to the marrow in my bones, where it used to call home

while others remember that i cannot give blood,
cannot have sex unprotected, cannot bleed out
in the wide open.

it means that above all else, i must figure out how to
remember that i am still here

while others figured out how to remember that i am
slipping away

and that i must dare to figure out how to figure out
how to squeeze every bit of juice left in this here
lifetime for me, lest i too forget to remember that
though i still have this virus, i also still have

a beautiful. chance. at living. a very. delicious life.

i write poems these days in my dialysis chair

for seventeen years
four and a half hours
three days a week

i dreamed of other places to be

- *sitting in a movie theater chair, maybe*
eating popcorn, sipping a large fruit-punch-flavored
sparkling water while my eyes ingested a storyline
that made me feel the world was safe, and
only wonder would find me in
my future

- *sitting in a lawn chair at the beach, maybe*
watching bottlenose dolphins disappear in the waves,
and my best friend disappear into yet
another mango margarita while my heart remembers
how delicious it is to play in the sunlight
with those i love

- *sitting in my boyfriends lap, maybe*
in his favorite blue recliner drinking in mimosas
and the cedar scent of his cologne
while my ears drink in his battleground stories of
how long it took him to finally
learn to love

and, sometimes, often
more than often

i dreamed i was

- on my deathbed, maybe
letting the last seconds of my life
tick away while my cells celebrate
the completion of this harrowing cycle
of showing up to a place i really
don't want to be, and
feeling less than how i know i
deserve to feel
while i do it

for seventeen years
four and a half hours
three times a week

this is how i spent my time
in a dialysis chair -

dreaming of some other place to be
rather than here

however,
these days

i no longer dream that life can only find me elsewhere

for i have found a way to grow it
right here

within the threads of this recliner

to water it while my blood drains away from me
through tubes, and my potassium drops down
towards the "acceptable" levels
and caregivers who have touched my body for
seventeen years but do not
even know my nickname, nor that the color that
makes me feel most relaxed is not this bland beige
plastered all over everything
tell me what would be best for me to eat
and drink, and do with the remainder of my life

i found a way to grow a life in a dialysis chair

i write poetry

while dialysis techs type my lab results onto my machine,
i type about what's been hurting

what's been healing
what's been missing, and then
longed for

i type about what i've learned
what i've seen

what i've lost and found and then
lost again

i type about love
and how elusive it's been

how forgetful/neglectful i'd been of it
when it finally walked itself to me out of the woods

i type about how i remembered that i am enough
how long i thought i wasn't
how terrible that period of forgetting was

i type about what has tried to take my life away
and how it's failed, gloriously
because i always find ways to bring it back

i type what i most need to hear

beauty, and possibility, and
healing, and second and third chances

and though i have not quite written for this entire
seventeen years

four and a half hours
three days a week

has recently been enough
for me to learn that
dreaming myself far away
from here

is only necessary when
what is here is not growing,
not nourished

writing poetry is
nourishing me

and dialysis has become the
place where i get fed

if that isn't a sign of the greater love:
that even in the midst of our own personal pain,
life will offer us slices of pleasure

that we do not have to leave where we are
to receive what we deserve

that heaven always knows how to find us,
even if we've hidden ourselves so deeply in hell

every morning

right after my feet hit the floor
from the softness of my bed

i lumber to the kitchen

slice a green apple
put a handful of blueberries in a bowl
scoop two tablespoons of
pumpkin seed butter from a jar
to the side of the blueberries in the bowl

make a cup of my favorite herbal tea
(at the moment)

and then sit myself down
to ingest

it's my favorite breakfast, this

because it tastes good to me

and i believe it to be highly
nutritious and nourishing

it feeds me

but

i do not feel properly full
until i have also eaten

love

until i have written a short list
of what i'm grateful for

until i've stood before the mirror
and looked into my own eyes
and celebrated + appreciated myself

until i've forgiven myself
and let something go from yesterday
that's too heavy to travel into my
today

until i've breathed deeply
and felt truly alive

in this body
in this day
in this life

i do not believe my body has been properly fed
or nourished

until i've eaten

love.

i do not dare enter a day
without it

i do not dare starve my body
of what it needs

188

to be well

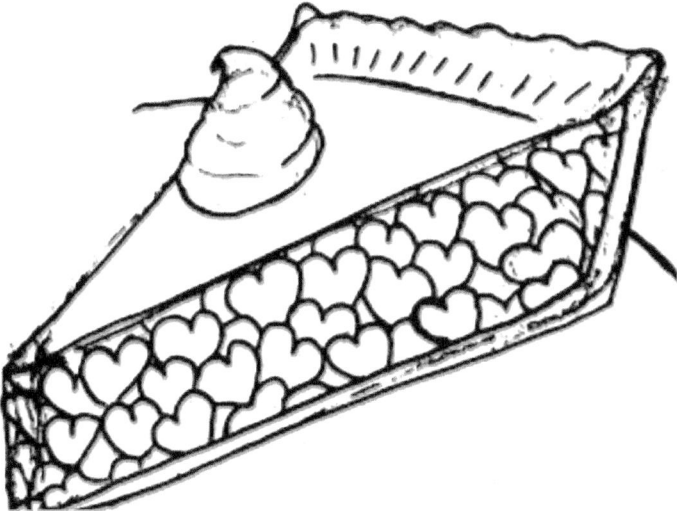

the day i got diagnosed

i remember how she walked me down the hall
louder than she should have been

to a room colder than it should've been

this way sir

limited eye contact

i can't remember if she was a nurse
or a case manager

or just an employee
who didn't have enough education
or experience, or passion

to be able to do what she really wanted to do

but what i could feel is that whatever that was
this wasn't it

have a seat sir

on a flat chair with no cushion
in a room with no color

didn't they know how soft the seats needed to be in here?

soft enough to catch the fall of someone's dreams
soft enough to hold their entire soul when it shatters

190

and lands in a million pieces on the cotton
and foam and upholstery and wood framing
beneath them

soft enough to keep those pieces whole
so that they could be offered back as seeds
to plant in soil later

to grow a different kind of life

so...ok....
you're hiv-positive

said with no fanfare, no light, no laughter or joy
no hug or bowl of my favorite
thing to eat

no warmth

just cold words, spoken on dying air

so cold they burnt
my skin when they touched it

leaving parts of me frostbitten

fearbitten

i think the only thing we should get to speak to
someone we think is dying is life

our words should feed them what we believe is lacking,
diminished, slipping away

i learned that day that we have forgotten how to be medicine

how to let our words be a sacred balm
when we are in the presence of someone who is
leaving home from wellness

now our tongues just offer more illness

we add more fear
more shame, more disconnection

we add more weight to a life that is already too
heavy for a journey that can only be survived by
traveling light

i deserved better
i deserved love

i deserved to be wrapped in the roots of the trees
waiting beneath the floorboards of the cement
foundation underneath my feet

until i remembered i am held

and that anything that is held can always
find its way back to being well

i deserved to be eating my mothers spaghetti and a
slice of my grandmothers pound cake to help me
wash down the words i'd never digest

i deserved to hear lizz wright playing over the loud speaker
repeatedly singing her beloved phrase
open your eyes, you can fly

until i remembered nothing i could ever hear
could rob me of my wings

i deserved to be told in warm words in a soft room that:

a virus might be able to take away my current plans,
but it could never take way my ability to dream for
a life that i could be proud of, could be alive in,
could find joy within

i deserved to be loved

but what i got was fear

and it has taken me a whole lifetime
since that day to regurgitate it so
that i have room in my gut for what i really need

more life

more life when i open these pill bottles, more life
when the needles poke me at the lab, more life
when my t-cells seem to be playing hide and seek,
more life when i disclose my journey to a stranger
because i do not want them to be so, any longer

since that day i have had to learn to speak life to me

to gulp it down, slurp it up
twirl it slowly with fork and spoon

ingest it with eyes wide shut

because what else could be more nutritious?
what else could be more worth it?

if this is to be my
last meal

then i want to eat life

please, while i'm dying
only feed me life

about the author

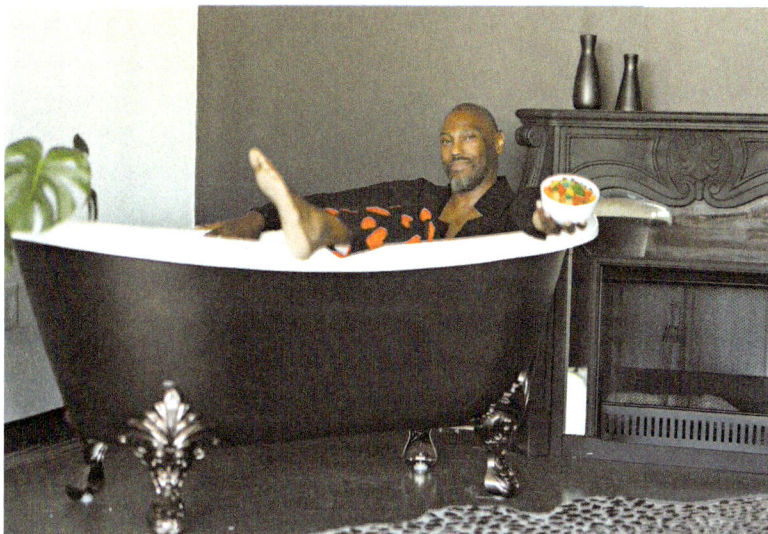

JEROME BRAGGS is an author based in oklahoma city, who believes that "*poetry is medicine, too.*" his poetry engages with themes of self-healing, relationships, spirituality and love. jerome shares his poems and writings with the world in an effort to create written and audible spaces for transformation and healing through self-love. His writings and live performances have touched thousands, and been featured in spaces around the world. when jerome is not writing, he is working as a medical intuitive hosting live workshops, sacred retreats, offering online courses, and working one-on-one with private clients, all teaching how to heal ourselves through the practice of self-love. You can find more of his work at: www.jeromebraggs.com